S U M O

MAKOTO KUBOTA

CHRONICLE BOOKS
SAN FRANCISCO

First published in the United States in 1999 by Chronicle Books.

Copyright ©1996 by Makoto Kubota, Libro Port.

Art Direction: Maki Iida (Heliopolis Inc.)
Editorial Direction: Fumihiko Tanji (Libro Port Co., Ltd.)
Introduction: Doreen Simmons
Text: Osamu Shimizu
Translation: ID Corporation, Hiromi Sakiyama, Gordon Fitzgerald

Design: Benjamin Pham

Printed in Japan.

ISBN 0-8118-2548-5

Library of Congress Cataloging-in-Publication Data available.

Distributed in Canada by
Raincoast Books
8680 Cambie Street
Vancouver, B.C. V6P 6M9

10 9 8 7 6 5 4 3 2 1

Chronicle Books
85 Second Street
San Francisco, California 94105

www.chroniclebooks.com

ALTHOUGH THE JAPANESE TRACE SUMO WRESTLING BACK TO LEGENDARY TIMES, IT HAS ONLY EXISTED IN THE FORM WE RECOGNIZE TODAY FOR ABOUT TWO HUNDRED YEARS. MANY OF THE TRAPPINGS OF PRESENT-DAY SUMO ARE TWENTIETH-CENTURY ARTIFACTS. NEVERTHELESS, THERE IS A STRONG SENSE OF CONTINUITY AND A CONSCIOUS—SOME MIGHT SAY SELF-CONSCIOUS—HARKING BACK TO SEVERAL STRANDS OF SUMO'S ORIGINS: AS A COURT CEREMONY, AS AN INTER-VILLAGE FESTIVAL TO PREDICT THE SUCCESS OF THE RICE CROP, AS PART OF A GENTLEMAN SOLDIER'S TRAINING, AND AS A MEANS OF EARNING A LIVING IF THE GENTLEMAN SOLDIER FELL UPON HARD TIMES AFTER HIS MASTER HAD BEEN DEFEATED IN WAR.

Sumo at its finest is a primal struggle—but with no forces of evil to overcome. Ideally, the good is pitted against the good. In a split second, the stronger and more skillful is decided. It is the ultimate in unarmed combat.

First-time spectators are impressed by the courtesies that precede and follow the explosive bout. A hand is raised in apology for passing in front of a judge. Bows are exchanged between winner and loser. Competitors bow to the sacred *dohyo* mound when entering and leaving and nod and hiss in polite greeting to a senior on the way to the changing room. Even in television interviews after a victory over the previous title-holder, the winner is quiet and diffident. While the interviewer struggles to find out if he had a plan of action when he entered the ring, the hero will often say no more than, "No, my mind was a complete blank. My body just followed through."

These courtesies are not empty forms. They have been instilled into every wrestler since his first day in the world of sumo. A new apprentice learns the basic rules quickly: keep yourself clean and neat, do not speak to a senior unless he speaks to you first, and if a senior gives you an order, jump to it! The days when apprentices feared to tread on their master's shadow are long gone, but the principle of respect remains. The *shin'ai,* a bamboo stick about the size of a fat

broom handle, is an important medium of instruction, in matters of behavior as well as technique. Seniors and the retired men who serve as trainers apply it generously to the wrestlers' buttocks and calves. Once a promising young man was struck by his stablemaster on the kneecap. He promptly quit, saying: "I will not serve a man who risks injuring his charges." In some stables, young men who need encouragement may also have sand or salt rubbed into their faces and stuffed into their noses and mouths. As in many sports, the old hands complain that the youngsters of today are spoiled and soft. They say they have no staying power and "they don't train enough and so they are injured easily."

Those who survive the early training, who learn to delve into their inner selves to find and unlock the latent power there, go on to great heights. Then, it is their turn to train others. There is seldom any viciousness in their treatment of their juniors. The "rod of kindness" is the only way they know to bring out the fighting spirit when it is needed.

Sumo aficionados are often asked why sumo wrestlers are so big. Quite simply, weight is an advantage. Few slender or lightweight men are successful in professional sumo's six divisions. But the talent scouts and stablemasters recruiting promising fifteen-year-olds as sumo apprentices are not looking for big fat boys. The ideal entrant is well built, taller than average, and has a deep chest and large broad feet, but is not noticeably fat. Obese boys who overeat and do not exercise cannot keep up with the rigorous sumo training and usually drop out within weeks. New recruits must start a regime that will continue until (and if they have any sense, for some time after) their retirement: rise at or before dawn, put on the cotton twill training belt (silk is for the top two divisions, and even for them only on public occasions), and, on an empty stomach, go methodically through a set of exercises to increase flexibility, strength, and endurance. After that, they move on to an hour's training in practice bouts.

Once through basic training, which lasts six months in the Japan Sumo Association's training school, a sumo wrestler is far more flexible than any ordinary member of the public. He can sit on the ground, stretch his legs out to the sides in a straight line, and bend forward until his face and chest touch the ground. Gradually getting to this stage involves a lot of pain—and the "kind" help of three friends: two with their own feet forcing his legs out and around into a straight line and the third, the heaviest, leaning or even sitting on his shoulders to force his chest down to the dirt.

Once the right movements have become second nature and the correct musculature has been developed, it is time to put on weight. Wrestlers eat plenty of rice accompanied by as much *chanko-nabe*—a stew of meat and vegetables—as they can consume. Occasionally, a beer-drinking session will be put on for the benefit of visitors, but in fact apprentices are not usually allowed alcohol. (Many of their seniors, however, are indeed renowned for their liquid capacity. Stories of gargantuan sessions with whiskey, beer, or sake, usually in a public challenge, are legion.)

The preparation of *chanko-nabe* is itself rooted in tradition. This stew consists of ten to twelve ingredients (more would begin to blur the flavors) boiled together in one pot or, in a sumo stable, a large metal vat. Originally, the basic protein was provided by chicken, fish, and tofu. According to old superstitions, eating four-footed animals would cause the sumo wrestler to fall down on all fours in the ring—an embarrassing way of losing. In these modern times, thin slices of pork or beef are often used. The other *chanko-nabe* ingredients are root and leafy vegetables.

While in itself *chanko-nabe* may not seem especially fattening, the schedule insures that the wrestlers will put on weight. Morning training on an empty stomach is followed by the *chanko* meal at noon, when the wrestlers are famished. After eating, they nap to ensure that the food moves more slowly through the digestive system. Some men with wastefully fast metabolisms resort to heroic measures when they have reached the top division and can make no headway without more weight. Some eat five huge meals a day. It is not only the occasional foreign entrant who has difficulty adjusting to *chanko*. The favorite foods of Japanese schoolboys are hamburgers and a very mild curry with rice. Indeed, many new apprentices actually lose weight in their first months.

The ideal sumo body is bottom heavy. There is no room in sumo for the "Mr. Universe" with overdeveloped shoulders tapering down to slim hips.

The area from waist to knees should have extra weight to give stability. The abdominal area, ideally, comes out in a firm *taiko-bara,* or "drum-stomach," to keep opponents at a distance. It also gives leverage to a man who can get a firm grip on his opponent's belt and then lean back, lifting his foe clean off his feet.

So how big are the wrestlers? The average height of the forty men in the top division in the March 1999 tournament was a little over six feet, but four men were under 5'10", and of those, one has won two championships and another has a record-breaking number of special prizes awarded for particular feats. The average weight was 352 pounds, with the heaviest man weighing 512 pounds and the lightest a mere 239 pounds. Attention often focuses upon the largest sumoist of all time, the now-retired Konishiki, as though he were the "typical" sumo wrestler. But he was born in Hawaii to West Samoan parents, and standing 6'1" (the average), he weighed at his maximum some 628 pounds. That is to say, he was a phenomenon, not a typical example. Incidentally, he has been married to a model for some years. Successful sumo wrestlers tend to marry extremely attractive women. There is certainly a glamour about these strong men, and not only for Japanese women. Most of those shown in this book are just such men—strong and successful. But here and there you will also catch glimpses of the hopeful juniors, the *gyoji* (referees), the *yobidashi* (callers), the *tokoyama* (hairdressers) and the many others who make up the unique world of sumo.

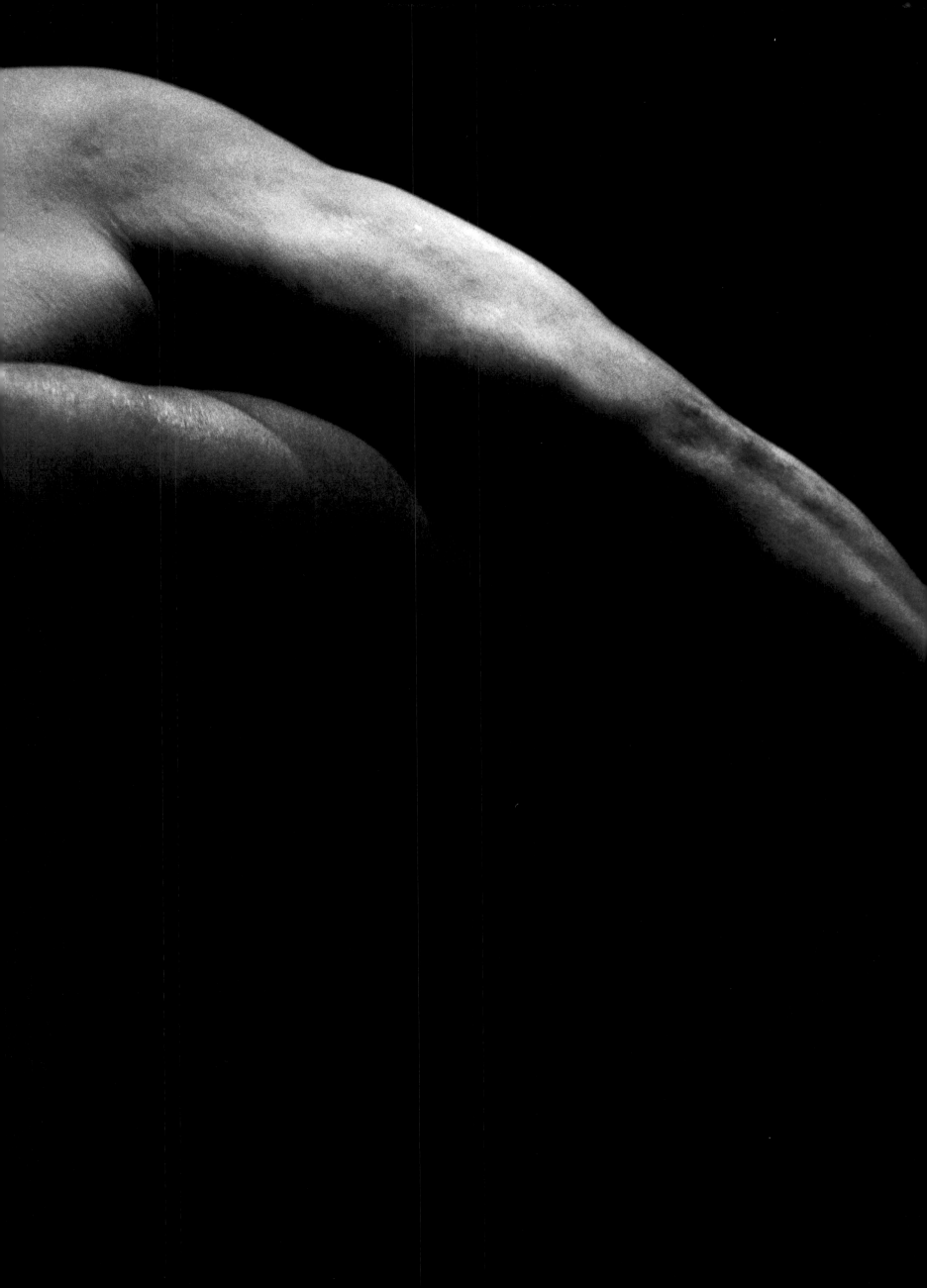

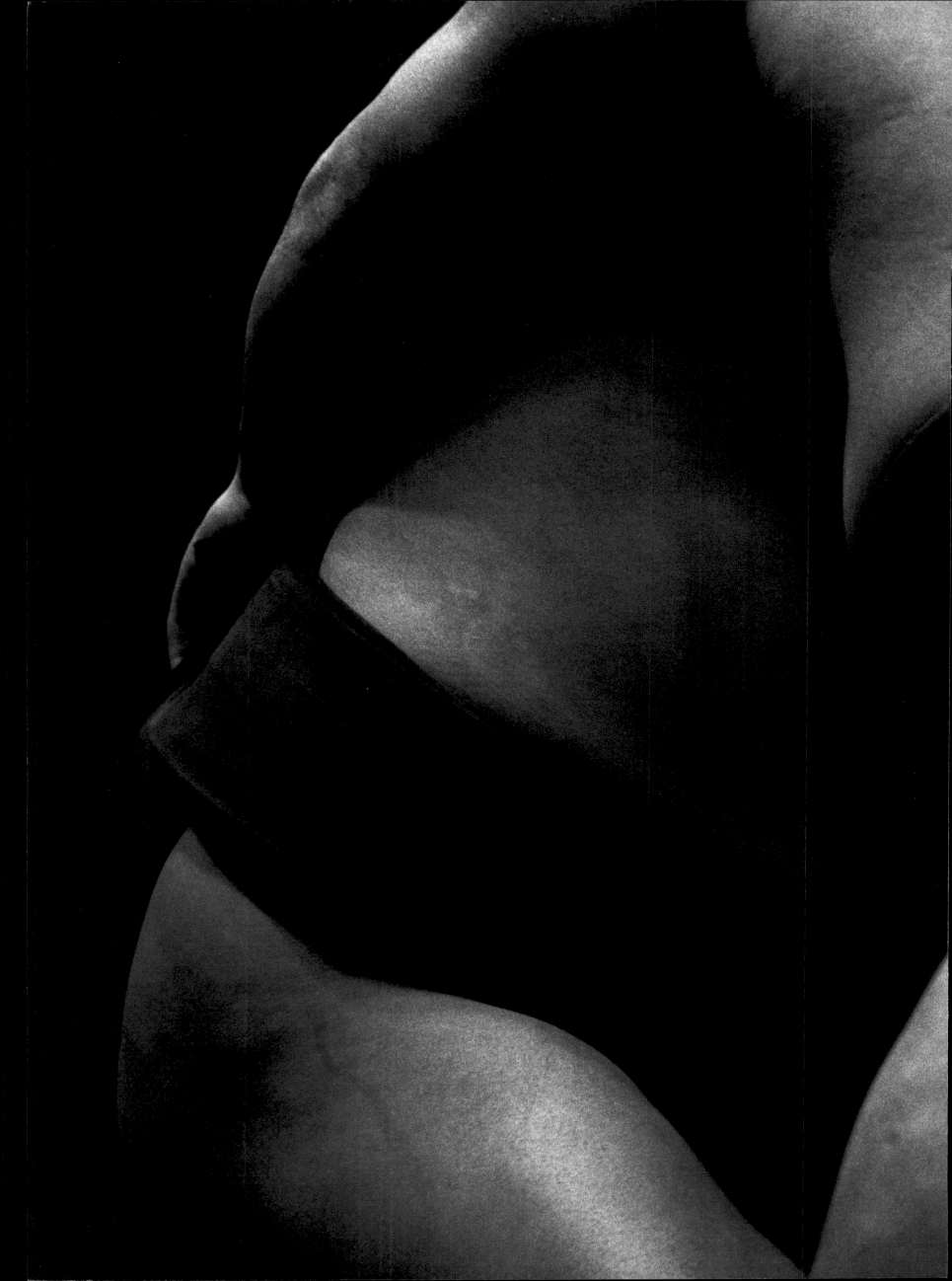

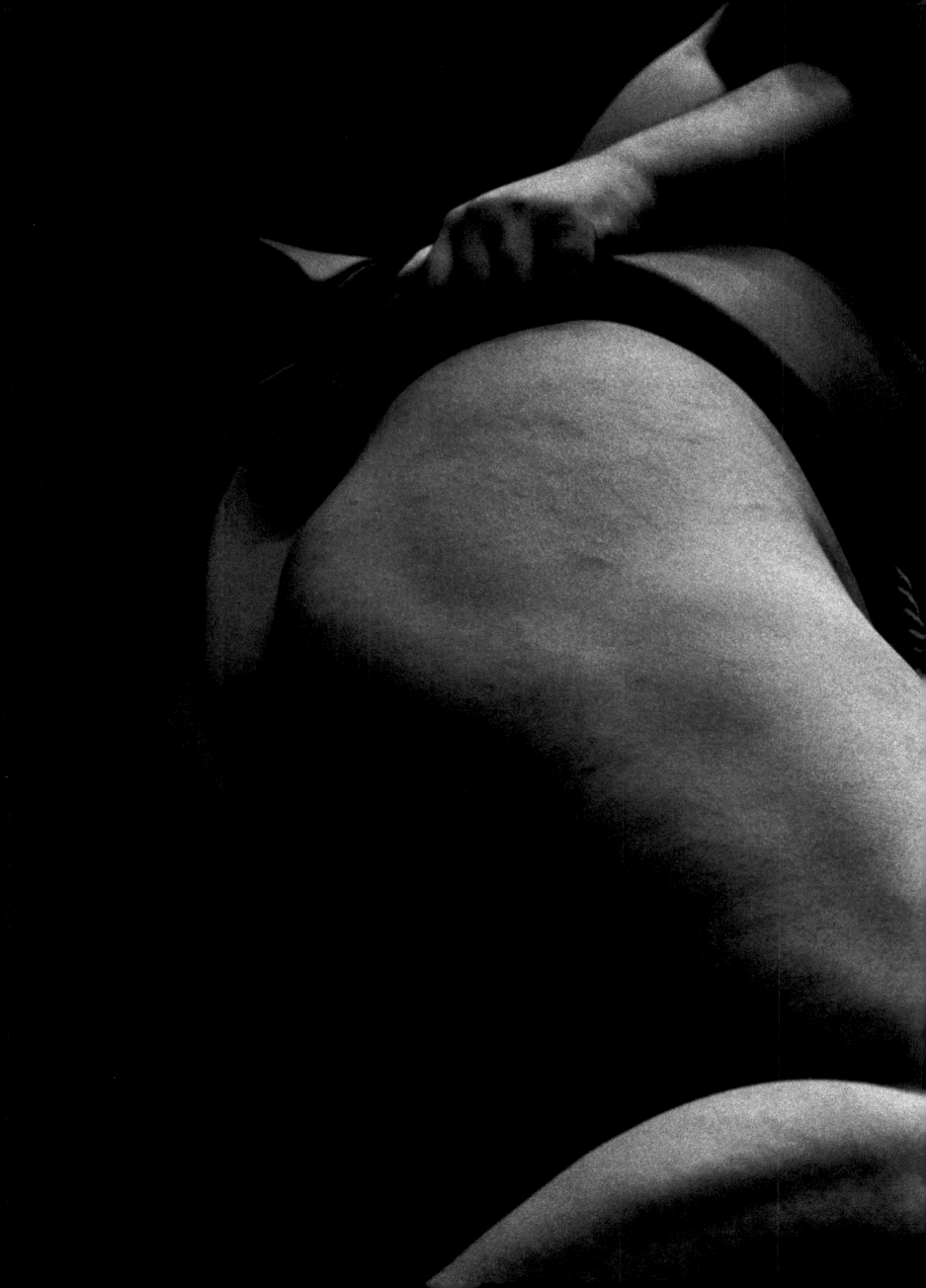

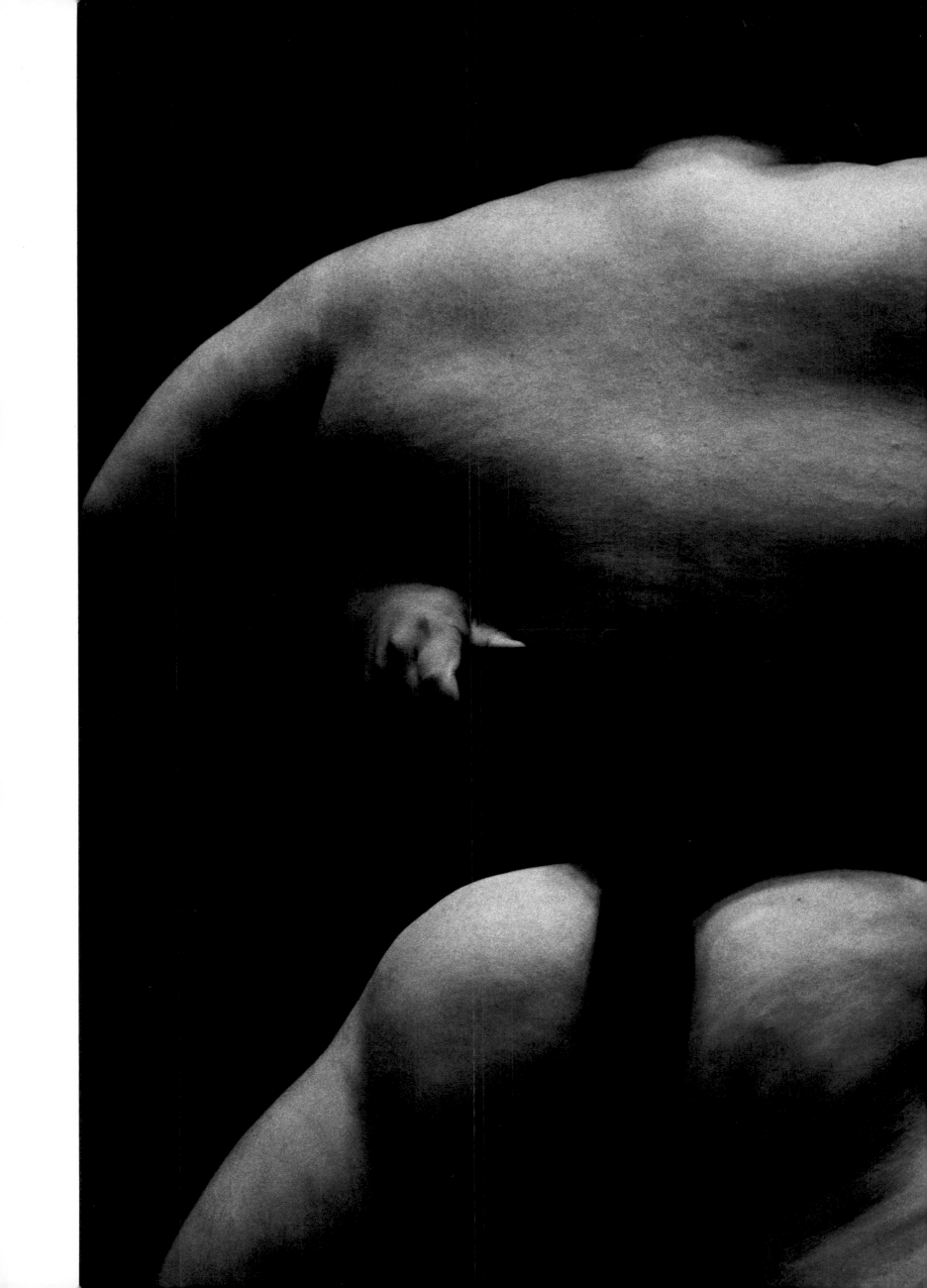

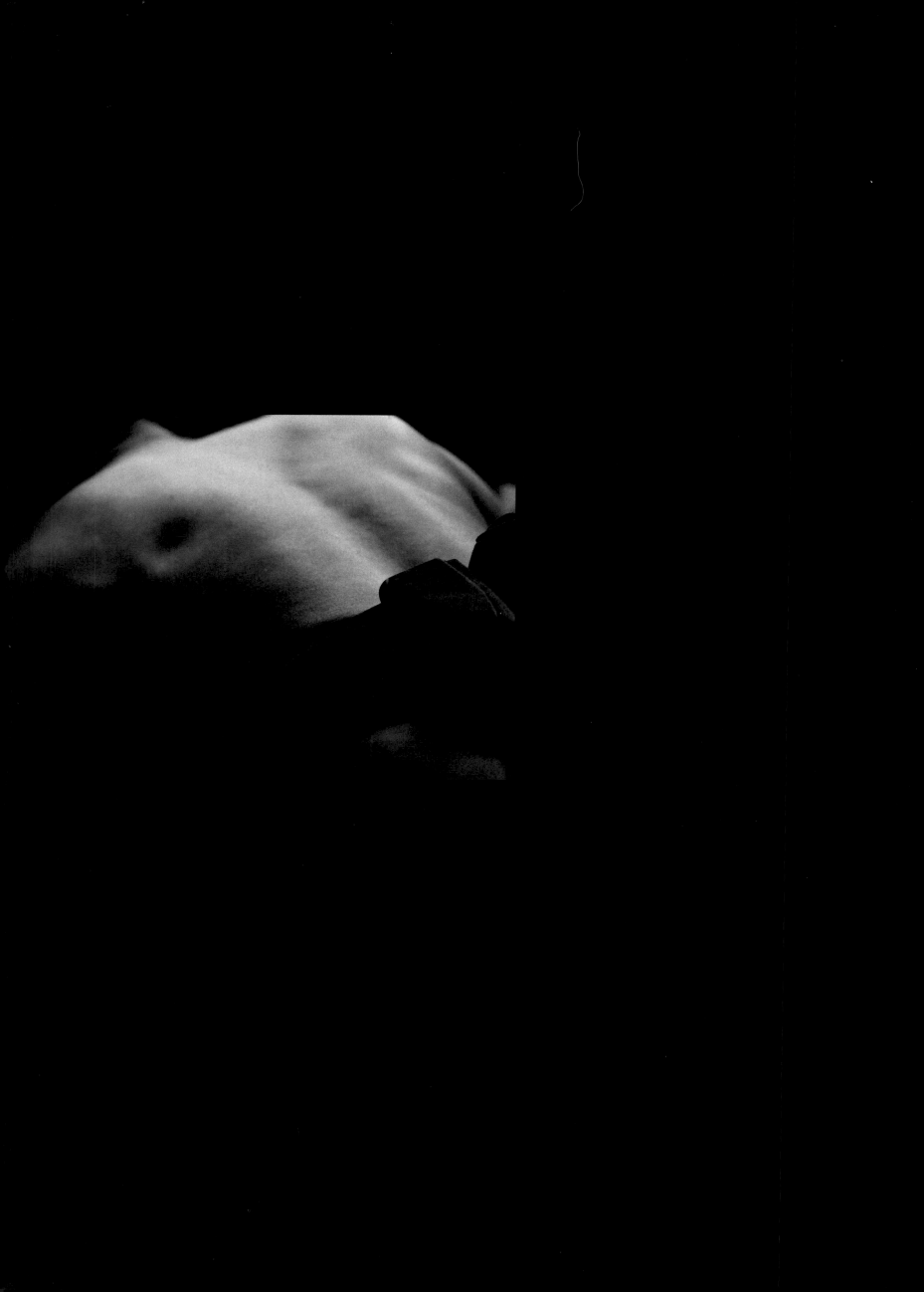

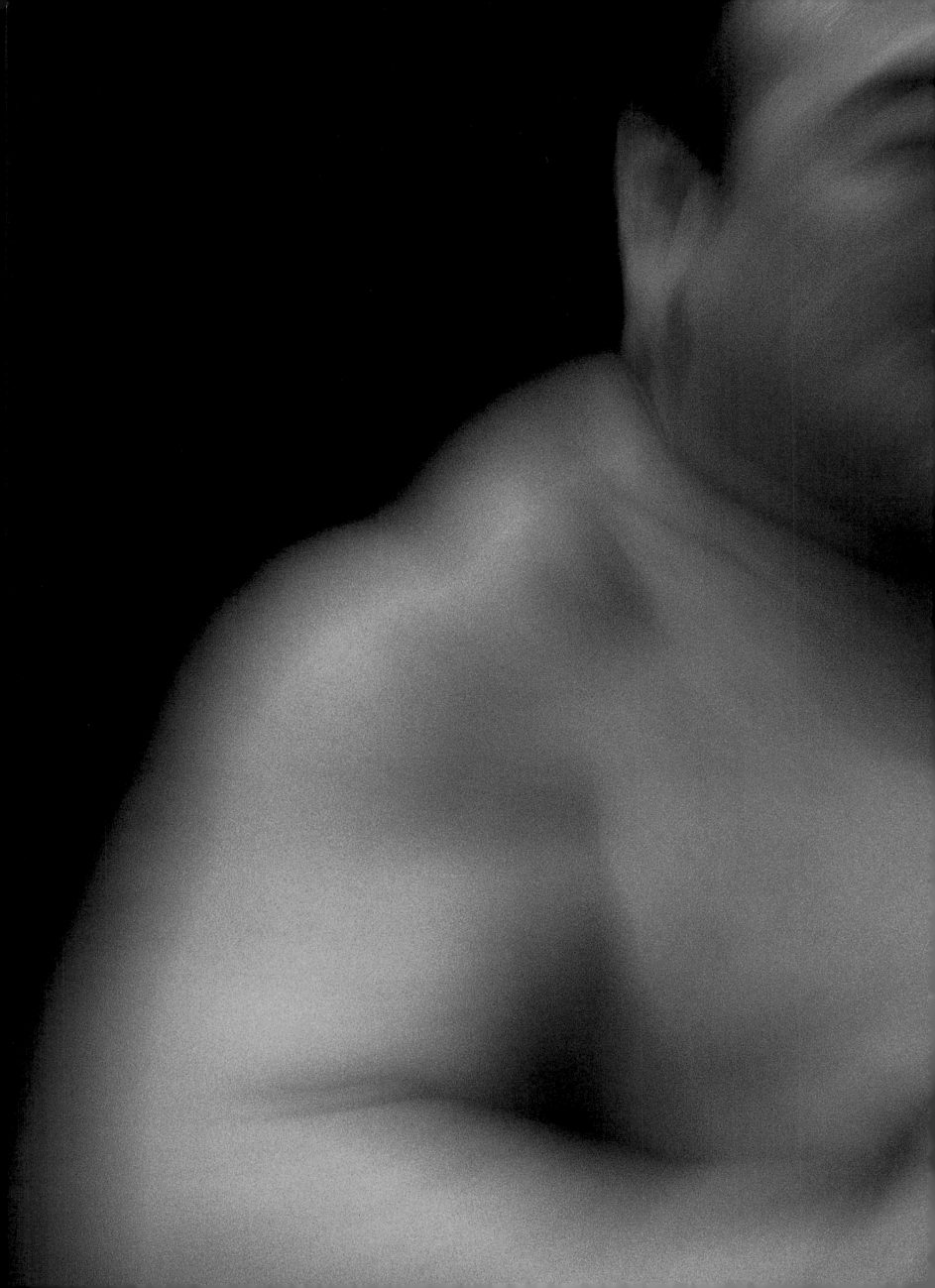

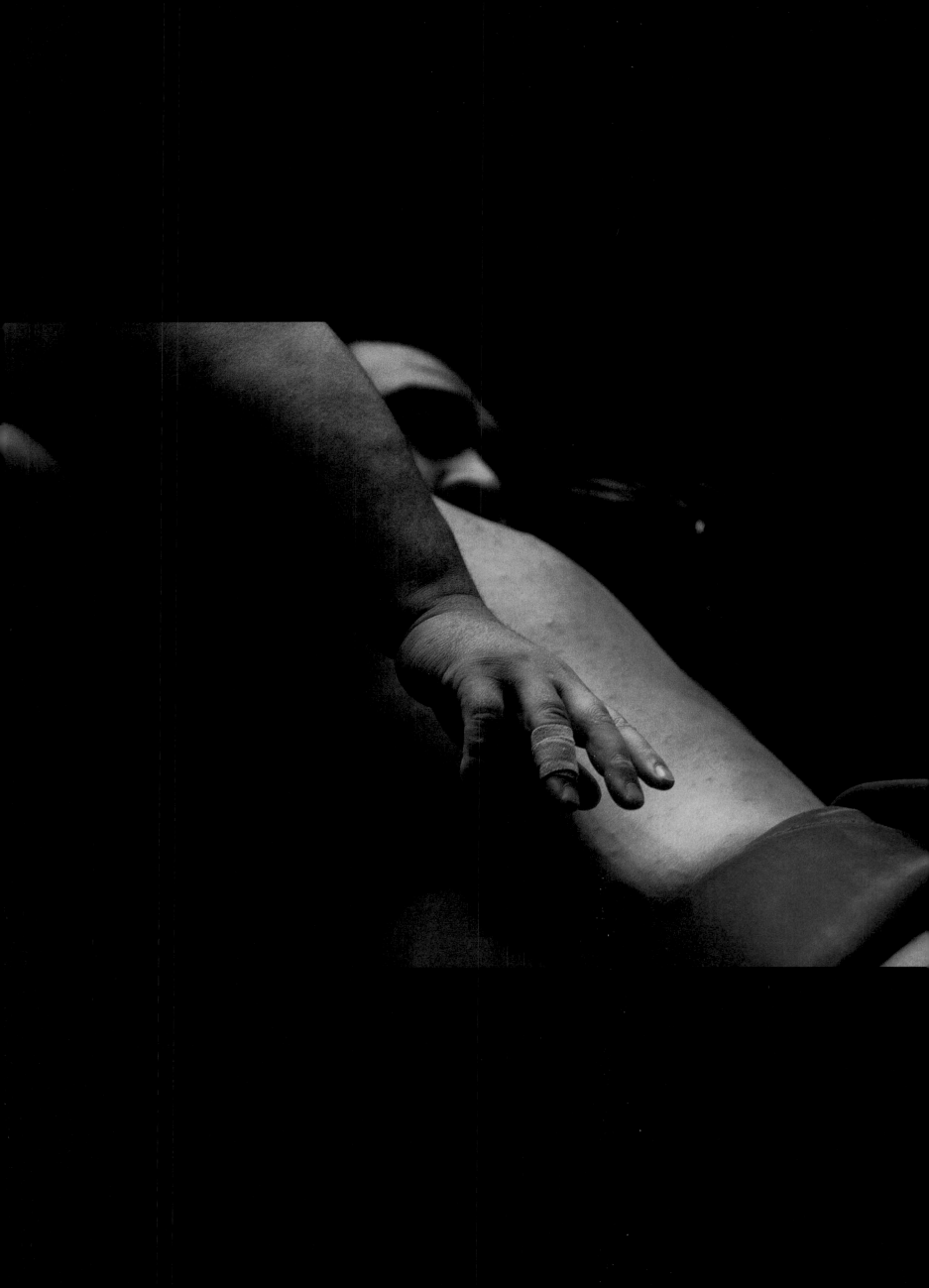

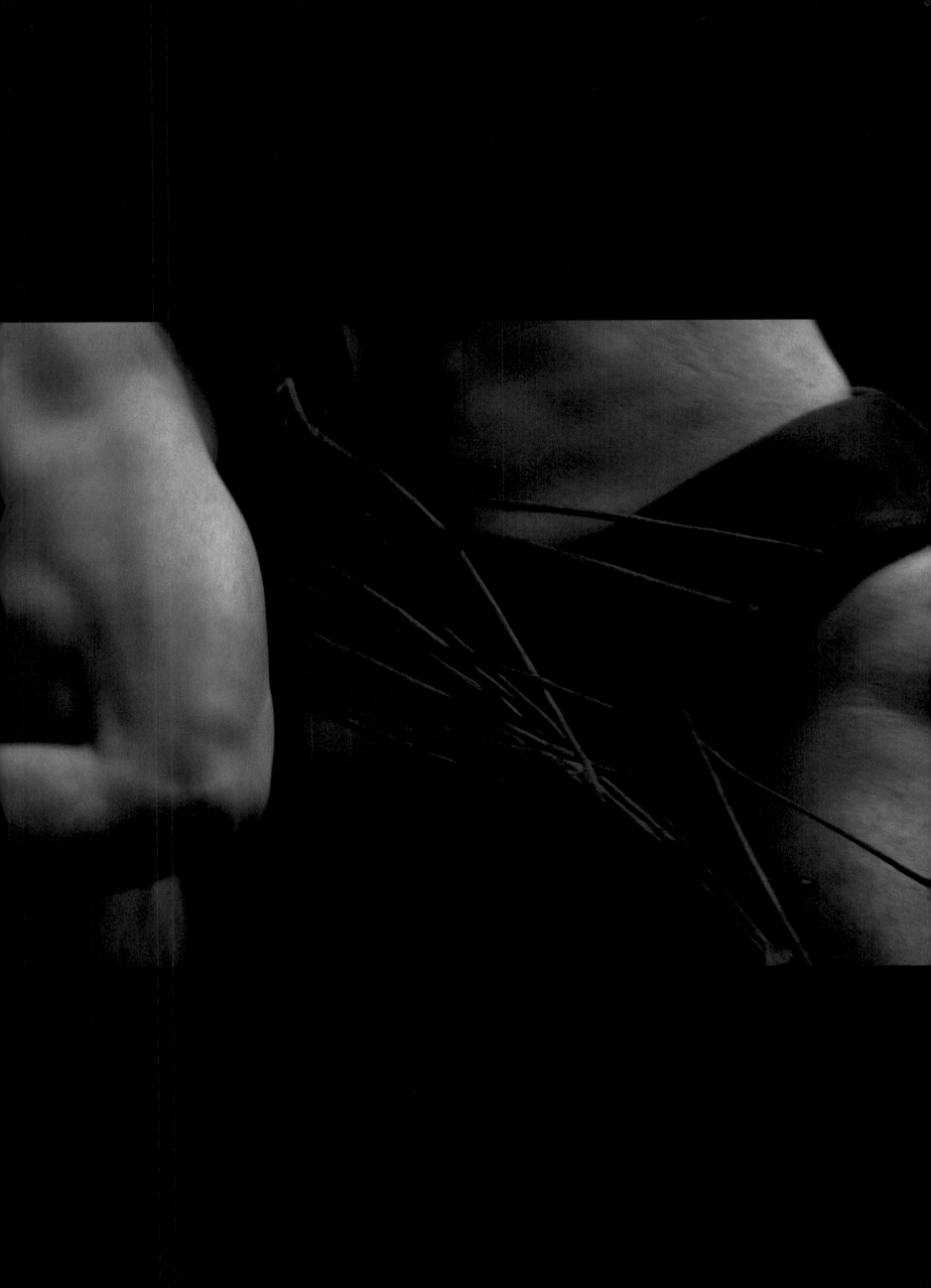

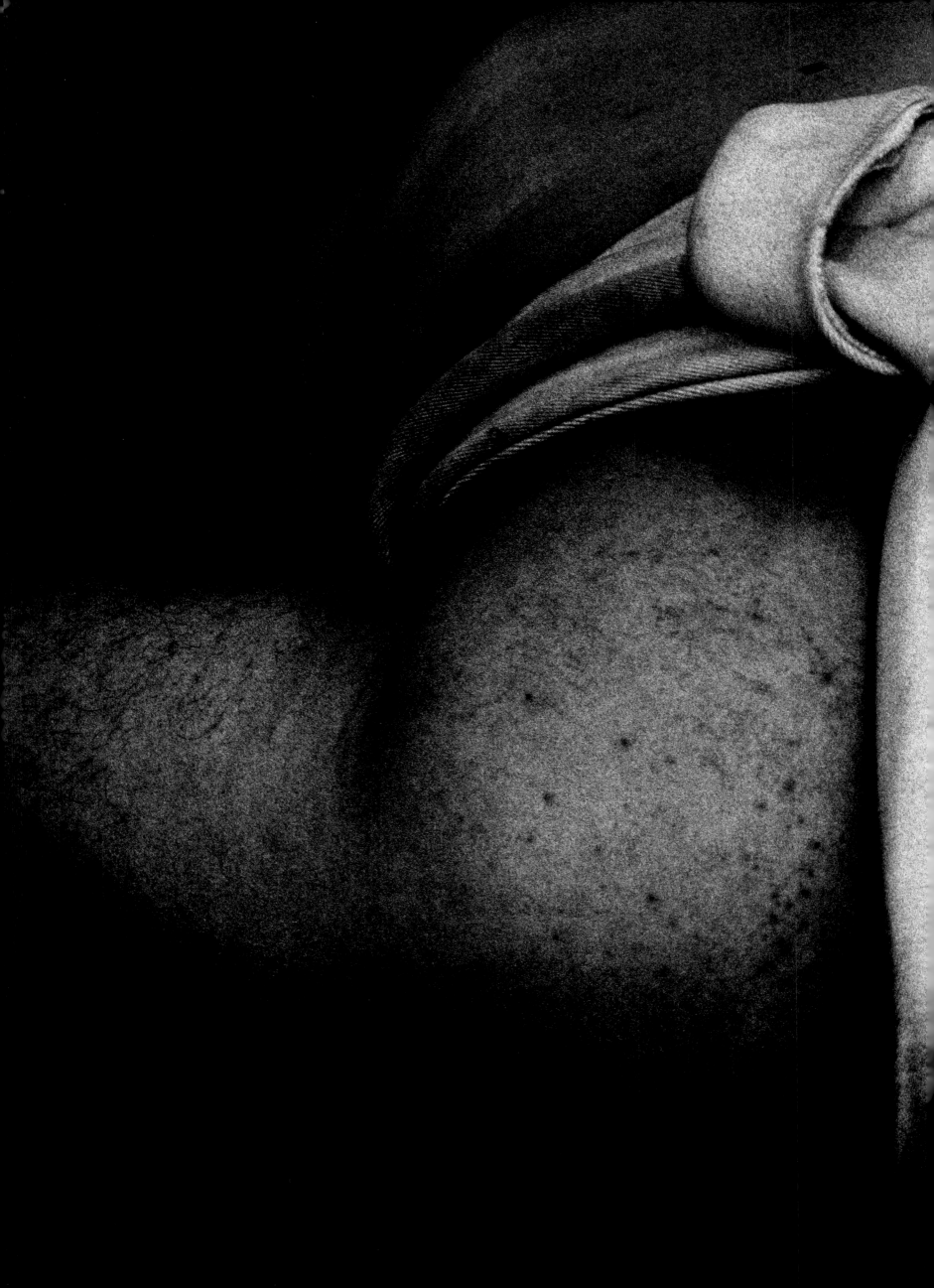

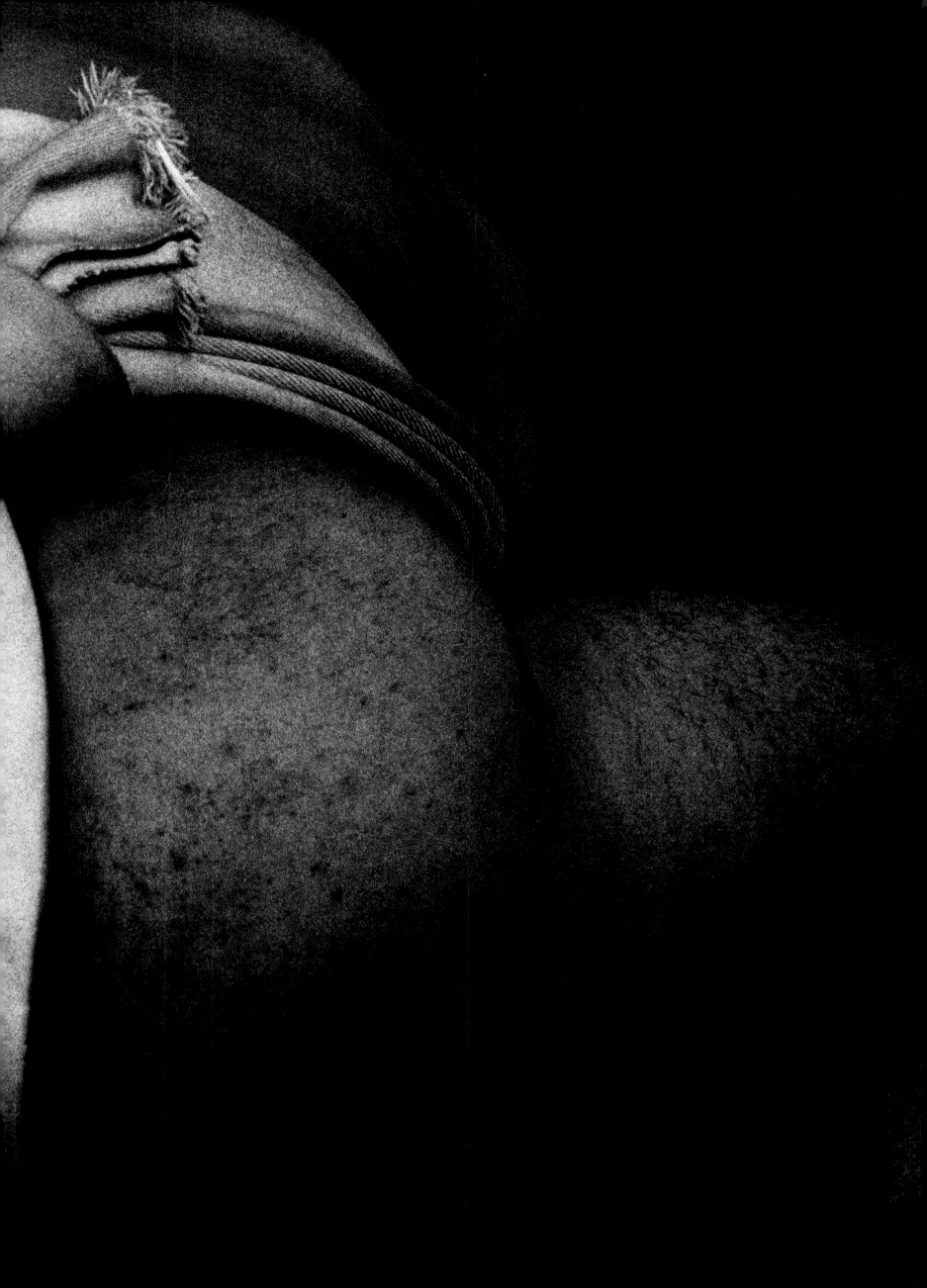

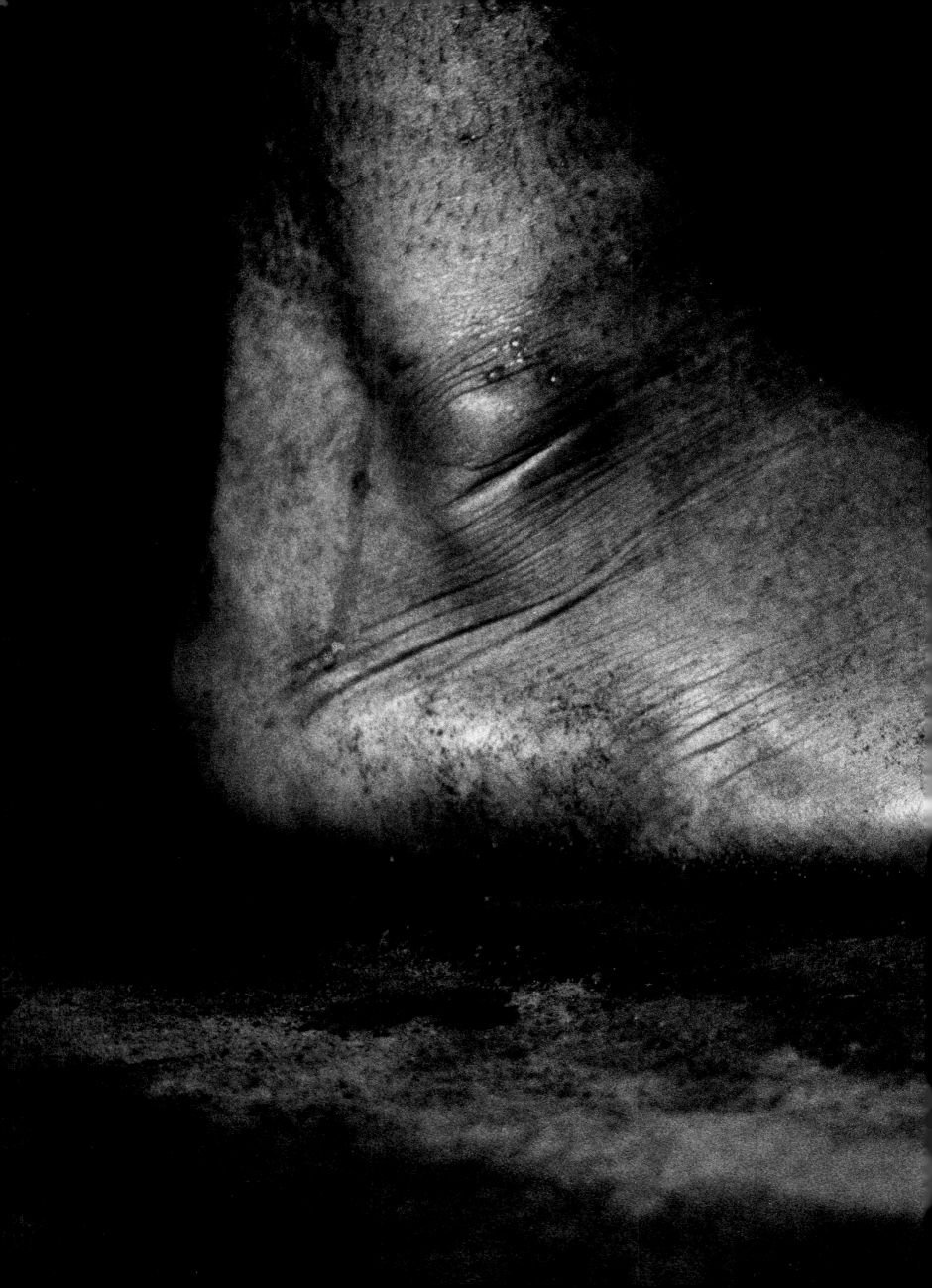

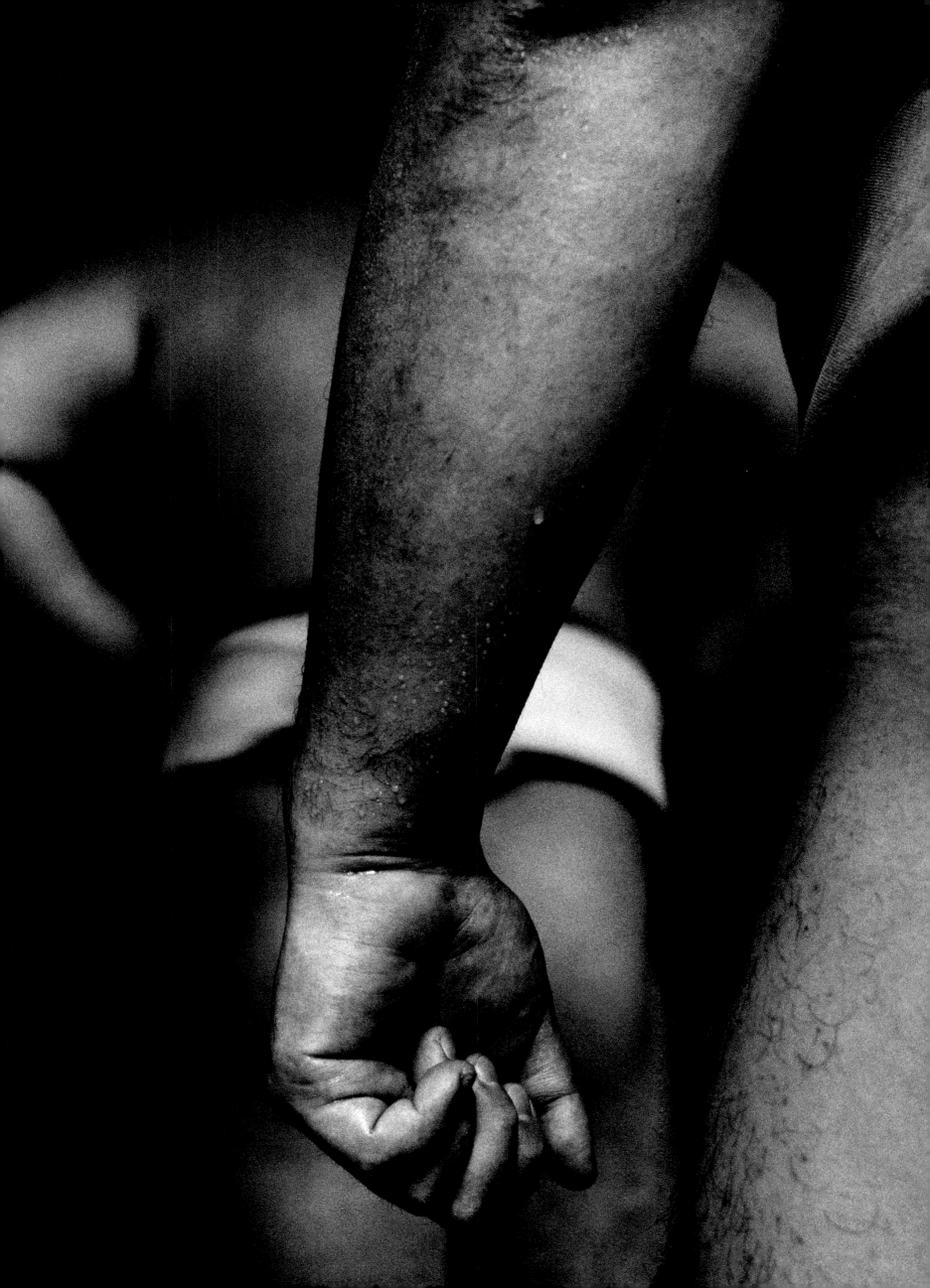

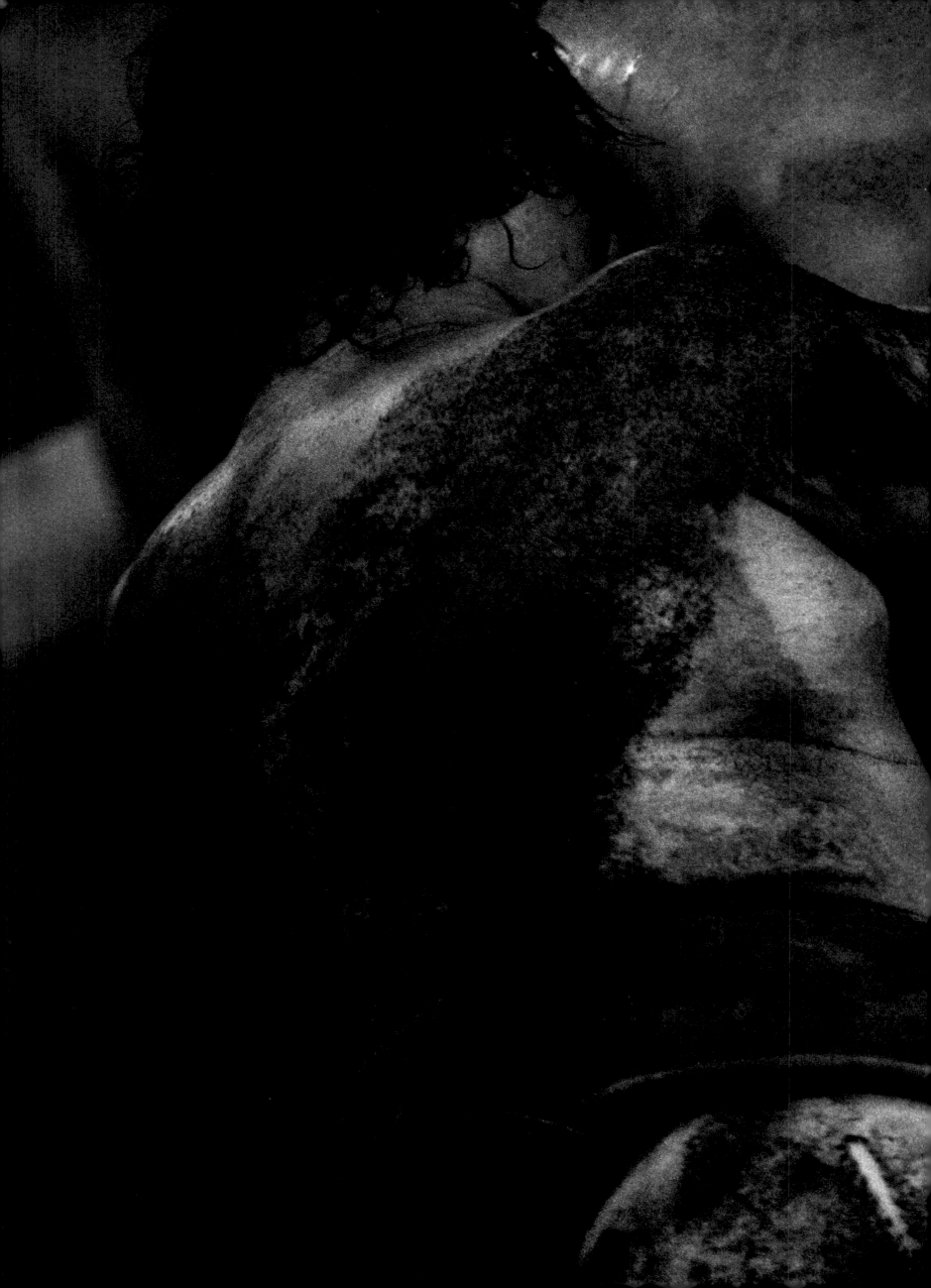

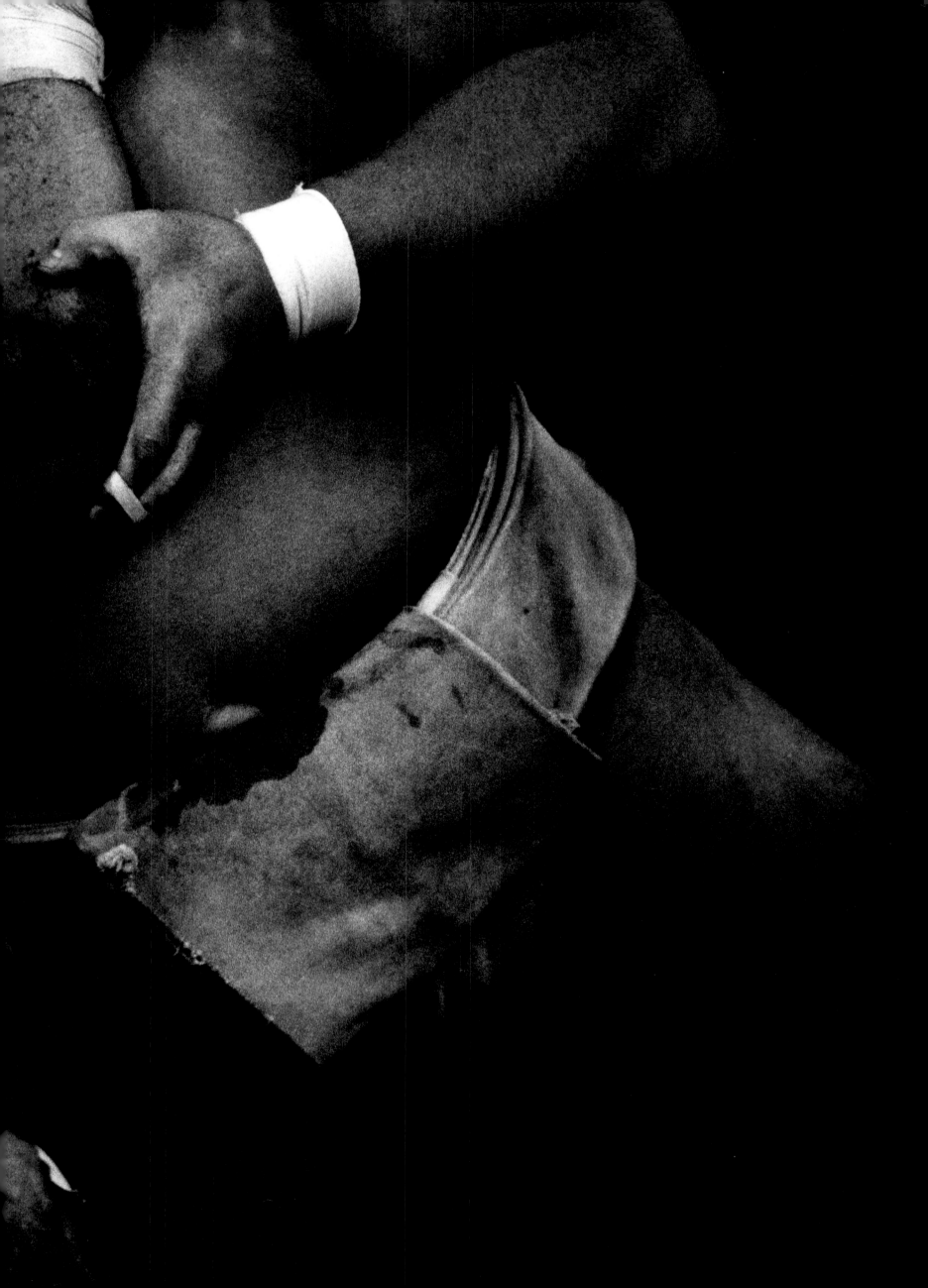

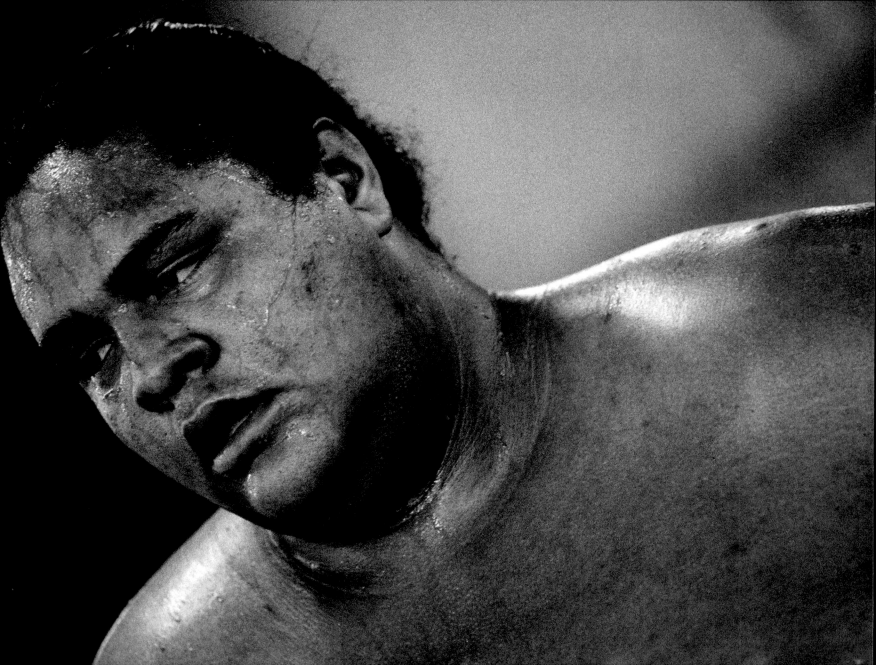

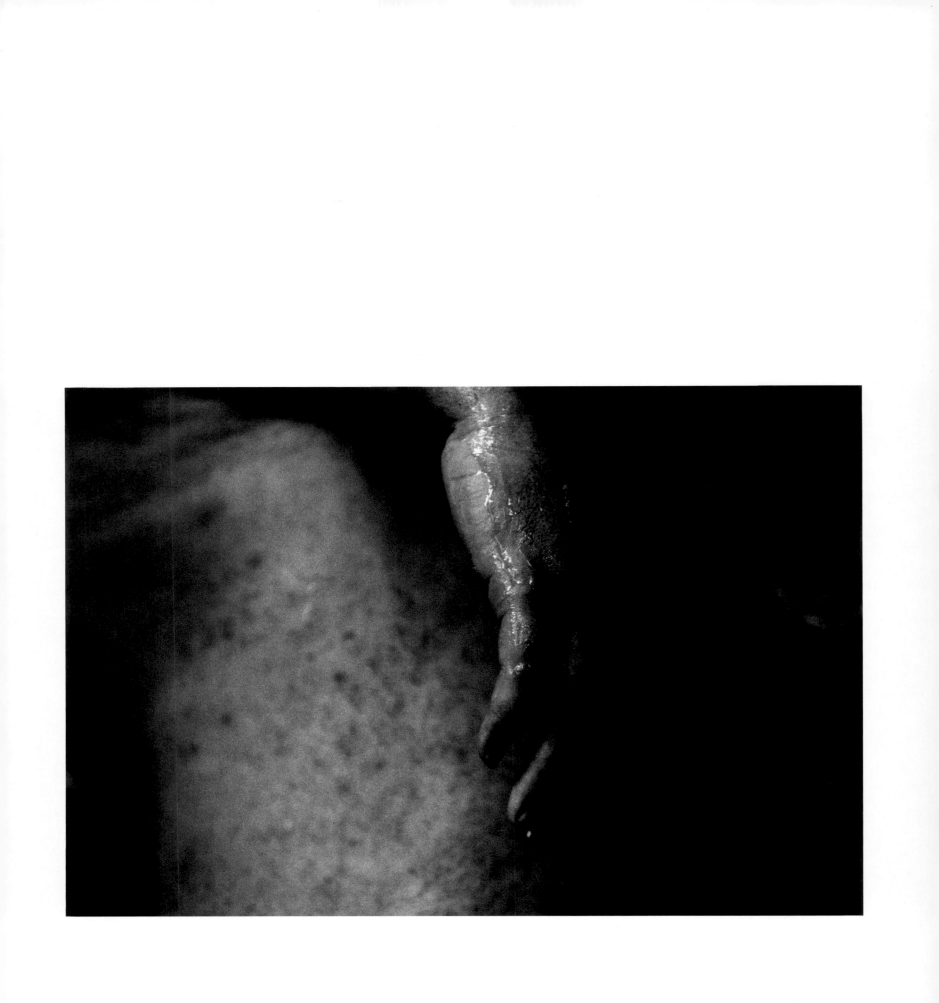

Long, long ago, there was a huge warrior, so strong he could throw down even demons. And there was another warrior, with tremendous mental toughness and powerful muscles. The two engaged in a test of combat to determine which was truly the strongest warrior, and onlookers were overwhelmed at the sight of them battling to the absolute limits of their strength. At the time, these two wrestlers were possessed of an almost supernatural strength and their exploits were so dazzling as to inspire awe.

Thus, sumo was born. The history of the wrestlers—*rikishi*—has continued to this day. Through a process of refinement—sometimes as a religious ritual, sometimes as entertainment—sumo has come to have a unique formal beauty. Sumo is both the martial art most familiar to the Japanese and a sacred ceremony.

TORIKUMI—THE MATCHUP
A STRUGGLE TO THE FINISH THAT LASTS MERELY SECONDS

Before the entire audience, the *rikishi* appear filled with an ardor to prevail in the battle. Ignoring the crowd, each wrestler rinses his mouth with *chikaramizu* to compose his spirit.(1) This *chikaramizu* means both "the water for cleansing the body before entering a sacred place" and "the last drink" before a fight to the finish. Then the *yobidashi* (match announcer) calls out the names of the *rikishi* in a loud voice.(2) The *rikishi* powerfully ascend to the *dohyo* (the ring) and begin to stamp on the clay with their feet, first one and then the other. These moves are called *shiko* and seem meant to drive away evil spirits.(4) After the *shiko*, the *rikishi* grab a handful of purified salt and fling it into the air.(5) The salt

traces a beautiful arc as it falls to the *dohyo*. The *rikishi* advance slowly to the center of the *dohyo*, then squat down and place both fists on the *shikirisen* (the starting line).(6) The two *rikishi* glare at each other with eyes meant to pierce their opponent. Then a feeling of calm returns to the arena. Following the moment of tension, the *rikishi* stand up and throw salt again. The *rikishi* repeat this *shikiri*—preparation for the bout—over and over, concentrating their mental and physical powers. When both wrestlers have pumped up their martial ardor to a peak, the *gyoji* (umpire) announces that the time for the bout has arrived.(7) There is a final *shikiri*, after which both *rikishi* strike the clay and stand.

The two *rikishi* then collide with such violent force that sparks seem to fly.(8) With their hands gripping the *mawashi* (belt) of their opponent, both wrestlers' faces turn bloodred. And then the instant of movement halts. Immediately afterward, though, the wrestlers unleash another furious attack until the battle is finally decided. It has all taken place in a few seconds. *Gunbai* (a fan) of the *gyoji* indicates the winner.(9) The two wrestlers exchange bows and depart the *dohyo*.

The rules of sumo are extremely simple: either force the opponent to the surface of the *dohyo* by throwing him off balance, or push him outside the *dohyo*(3), a ring about 4.55 meters in diameter. These are the only two standards for victory or defeat. The enormous *rikishi* compete in a relatively tiny *dohyo*. The techniques and moves for winning are worked out within these limits. These are the forms called

10

11

the *shijuhatte* (the forty-eight moves), classified into *tsuki* (thrusts), *oshi* (pushes), *nage* (throws), and *kake* (hooking trips). There were more than three hundred techniques in the Edo period, but these have now been classified into about seventy types of attack. All of the *rikishi* undergo strenuous training every day to build up their physical strength and refine their techniques.

The short length of the bout is the most significant feature of sumo as a martial art. Compared to wrestling and boxing, the length of the bouts is indeed extremely short. Actually, though, a sumo bout is already under way while the *shikiri* is being carried out, when the energy within the *rikishi* is gradually built up in order to explode during the *tachiai*.

But sumo is not simply a fight to the finish. It is a ceremonial ritual in which noble strength is consecrated.

13

14

15

12

YOKOZUNA

THE COMBATANTS CLOSEST TO THE GODS

The *yokozuna,* the *rikishi* at the pinnacle of sumo, are the *rikishi* selected to head the East and West sides, one to each.(10) The *yokozuna* conducts a special ritual wearing a large *tsuna* (rope), from which the word *yokozuna* is derived.(11) There are two ceremonial styles according to how the rope is tied, the *unryu* style and the *shiranui* style. The former has a shape in which one bow stands vertically, representing a turtle walking the earth. In the latter, two bows are tied together, signifying a crane taking to the air. The ropes representing the pair of the crane and the turtle, a symbol of happiness, are a Japanese form of artistic expression. Although ropes are sometimes used to indicate a sacred precinct, such as in a Shinto shrine, in this case they show that the *yokozuna* is a presence close to the gods. There is no demotion from the rank of *yokozuna*. The *yokozuna* is an absolute presence whose position is assured until his retirement. This is proof of the warrior's glory.

16 17

18

TRADITIONAL ENTERTAINMENT AND SUMO

The sumo schedule consists of six main *basho* (tournaments) and four regional *jungyo* (performances) each year. The main *basho* begins with a *yose daiko* (a drum announcing the beginning of the tournament) at 8:00 A.M., and proceeds with bouts between lower-ranking wrestlers.(12) The *yokozuna* make their appearance around 6:00 P.M. After all the matches are completed, the *yumitori shiki* takes place.(13) This is a ritual performance proclaiming the winner of the final match of the day. The victorious *rikishi* waves a bow over his head and twists it around his body. This may seem an unusual performance by the *rikishi,* who are proud of their strength. This waving of a bow, however, is not unique to sumo. It is commonly seen in ceremonial rites in the Imperial court and festivals and dedications at shrines, and came to be incorporated into sumo ceremonies as well.

Many entertainments that cannot be seen in the main *basho* may be enjoyed in the provincial performances. One of these is *shokkiri*.(14) This consists of a comical explanation of sumo rules through rare techniques and violations of the rules by two *rikishi* from divisions lower than *makushita*. Then comes *sumo jinku*(15)—original melodies sung by *rikishi,* who are always proud of their voices, that are actually folk songs evoking the joys and sorrows of the *rikishi* and the outstanding points of the places they visit. These elements of performance show the deep relationship between sumo and indigenous popular entertainment.

19

20

21

21

SACRED GROUNDS

THE *DOHYO* AND SUSPENDED CEILINGS

For the main *basho,* a new *dohyo* is created by *yobidashi* for each tournament. A *dohyo* festival is always conducted for the new *dohyo.*(16) On the day before the first day of the tournament, the center of the *dohyo* is decorated with sacred strips of paper and *sakaki,* a sacred Shinto tree, and offerings of liquor and the fruits of the seas and mountains. The *gyoji,* dressed in the robes of a shrine official, then offers a prayer of invocation, and the food is buried in a hole dug in the center of the *dohyo*. This offering is to appease the gods of the earth. Finally, sacred sake is poured on the *tokudawara,* which concludes the *dohyo* festival. This ritual purifies the *dohyo* and prevents demons from intruding therein. Sumo as a sacred ritual hereby takes place in a totally sacred place from which all evil has been banished.

The suspended roof that hangs above the *dohyo* is another sacred component of the sumo venue.(17) This roof follows the traditional architectural style of Japanese Shinto shrines. The four strands of braided fringe that hang from this roof represent the four directions and the four seasons, and the sacred animals that protect them. The seasons and the directions are kept out by these four braids, and the center is considered a sacred place.

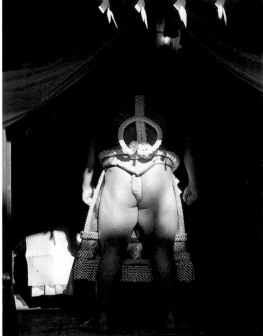

THE *GYOJI* AND *YOBIDASHI* AS SCENE MASTERS

The *gyoji* judges the winner of each bout and oversees the wrestlers' progress. He also has another extremely important role—writing the Japanese characters in the style unique to sumo events, called *sumo-ji,* that is used for writing the *shikona* (the fighting names of the *rikishi*) on the rankings table and bulletin boards.(18) These *sumo-ji* are closer to drawings or designs than ordinary characters.(19) They are a sort of special typography and a major element supporting the formal beauty of sumo.

The main job of the *yobidashi* is calling out *shikona* of the *rikishi* before each *torikumi* (match). But they also have other important roles. One of these is *yagura daiko*(20)—the special technique for the *taiko* drum that has been handed down over the generations to announce the start of sumo events. Another is *dohyo tsuki,* the making of the *dohyo* itself. It takes about twenty *yobidashi* working for three days to make the *dohyo* for a main *basho.*(21)

THE ORIGINS OF SUMO

About sixteen hundred years ago, the emperor suggested a test of strength between a fierce warrior from Taima village named Kehaya, and a strongman named Sukune, who hailed from Izumo. The winner would be given a domain of land and guaranteed a position as a lieutenant to the emperor. The two men faced off. The tension was unbearable. Then both men raised their feet at the same time and plunged them through the body of their

opponent. Sukune's foot broke a rib bone of Kehaya. His posture broken, Kehaya fell to the ground. Then, without a moment's delay, Sukune crushed Kehaya's hipbone. The winner was Nomi no Sukune. Taima no Kehaya, with his pulverized hipbone, expired shortly thereafter.

In ancient times, sumo was called *sumai*—meaning "performing with nothing in one's hand." This was originally a performance intended to appease the souls of the dead and evil spirits. According to literature, the word *sumai* first appeared in the aforementioned legend of Kehaya and Sukune in the *Nihon Shoki*. This has been passed down as the origin of sumo, a legend that appears to be about two men's cruel battle to the death. But there is another significance concealed within this legend. The stamping of these two was the behavior that led to *shiko*. In ancient days, both *shiko* and stamping the ground had the connotation of driving away evil spirits. Having adopted *shiko,* sumo was conducted as a religious ritual to drive away evil and summon good fortune. Later, during the Heian period, it took root as a court ceremony. Meanwhile, the local character of sumo developed as a part of the harvest festivals. Although it was in decline for a time, sumo enjoyed the patronage of generals and warriors from the Kamakura period to the Warring States period. In the Edo period, *kanjin sumo* held by Buddhist temples flourished and became a popular entertainment, enjoyed by men and women regardless of age. During this long period of evolution, the culture of sumo has naturally fused into the minds of the Japanese.

From the genesis of sumo, the Japanese have always perceived its sacred nature. Whether it is enjoyed as a martial art or as a festival, it is revered throughout the land. Perhaps this is because the Japanese can see the gods and the spirit of nature in this age-old tradition.